RACE TO THE
MOON

Steve Parker

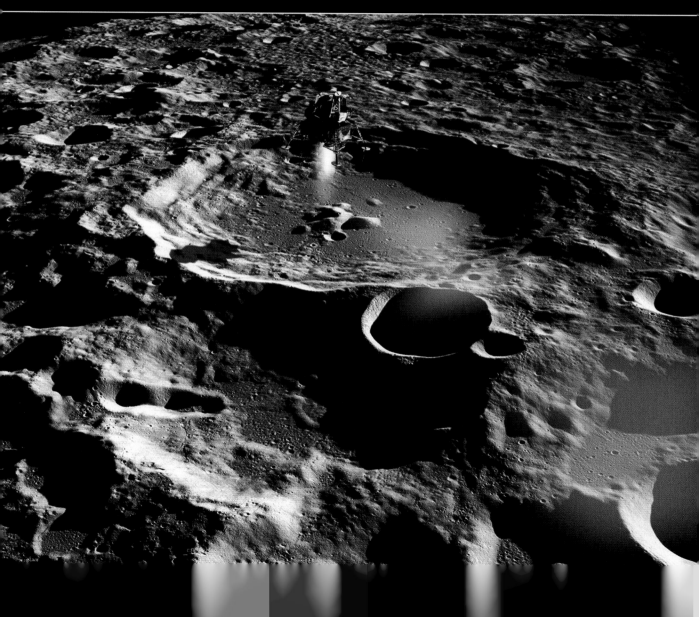

Published by Smart Apple Media, an imprint of Black Rabbit Books
P.O. Box 3263, Mankato, Minnesota 56002
www.blackrabbitbooks.com

Produced by David West 👥 Children's Books
6 Princeton Court, 55 Felsham Road, London SW15 1AZ

Designed by Gary Jeffrey

Library of Congress Cataloging-in-Publication Data

Cataloging-in-Publication Data is available from the Library of Congress.
ISBN 978-1-62588-078-9

CSPIA compliance information: DWCB14FCP
011014

9 8 7 6 5 4 3 2 1

All images courtesy of NASA except: p4-5, NASA/Astronaut Ron Garan; p11t, NASA/LOIRP, p11b, NASA Ames/Dana Berry; p12l, tr, b, Ebs08, p12m, Eberhard Marx

Saturn S-IV stage, accelerating to over 24,000 miles per hour (38,624 km/h) to break free of Earth's gravity. The Apollo spaceships are the only human-carrying craft to travel to another world.

INTRODUCTION

For centuries, humans gazed up at the Moon and wondered: What would it be like to visit? Low on the horizon, our one and only natural satellite seems magnified and close enough to touch. But it lies a far-flung average of 238,855 miles (384,400 km) away.

By the mid 1960s, spaceflight technology managed to bridge that immense gap with orbiting and landing probes. It would take superpower rivalry, the most powerful rocket ever made, and a group of intrepid heroes ready to risk it all, to finally get humans on the Moon.

Apollo 8's 1968 Moon-orbiting mission was the first time humans had been close to its surface. The crew scouted for sites for the following year's landing.

MOON DREAMS

By 1961 the first object, first animal, and first human into orbit had all been sent by the Soviet Union. National pride led US leaders to up the stakes and bid to be first to the Moon.

MOONSTRUCK

On May 5, 1961, Alan Shepard took a 15 minute sub-orbital "hop" in his Mercury capsule. He became the world's second man into space and the US's first astronaut. Five months earlier, US President John F. Kennedy had been elected partly on a promise of delivering American superiority over the Soviets in space exploration.

A US Moon mission, Apollo, was penciled in to follow the Mercury program. But little had been done. Kennedy believed the US *would* catch up and overtake the Soviets, given enough time. He recognized that Apollo was ambitious enough to fit the bill.

Jules Verne's 1865 science fantasy novel From the Earth to the Moon *imagined astronauts flying to the Moon in a projectile fired from a huge cannon.*

All we knew of the Moon was through telescope observations, like this map from 1886. The rotation of the Moon is synchronized with Earth's rotation, meaning the far side is never visible.

The idea of landing on another world seemed fantastical in the 1950s—the stuff of science fiction, not technological fact. Every stage, from launch rockets to landing vehicles, would be invented from scratch.

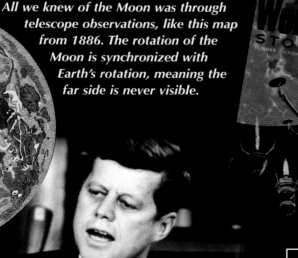

JOHN GLENN was the first **American** to **ORBIT EARTH**, on February 20, **1962**.

Kennedy addressed Congress on May 25, 1961. He stated his administration's goal of landing a man on the Moon by the end of 1969. Kennedy would not live to see it happen, but his bold commitment underpinned the whole Apollo project.

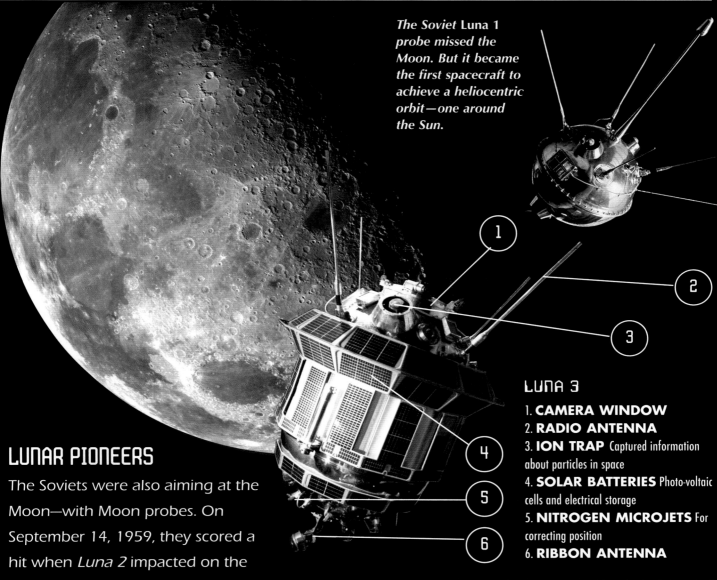

The Soviet Luna 1 probe missed the Moon. But it became the first spacecraft to achieve a heliocentric orbit—one around the Sun.

LUNA 3

1. **CAMERA WINDOW**
2. **RADIO ANTENNA**
3. **ION TRAP** Captured information about particles in space
4. **SOLAR BATTERIES** Photo-voltaic cells and electrical storage
5. **NITROGEN MICROJETS** For correcting position
6. **RIBBON ANTENNA**

LUNAR PIONEERS

The Soviets were also aiming at the Moon—with Moon probes. On September 14, 1959, they scored a hit when *Luna 2* impacted on the surface, scattering small metallic pennants inscribed with the Soviet coat of arms. One month later *Luna 3* swung around the Moon carrying a state-of-the-art camera and a fax machine-like scanner. As the camera passed over the sunlit far side, a light cell triggered the shutter. The film developed automatically, was scanned, and transmitted line by line when *Luna 3* came in view of Earth. It solved the first lunar mystery— what was on the far side of the Moon.

Pioneer 4, the fifth US attempt to probe the Moon, failed, but it became the first US object to escape Earth's gravity as it shot into space.

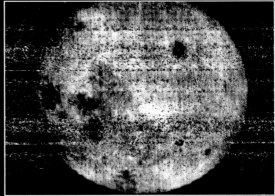

Luna 3 captured the first-ever image of the Moon's far side. It revealed a heavily cratered, mountainous surface, in contrast to the much flatter near side visible from Earth.

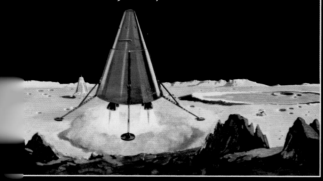

Early NASA ideas for Apollo imagined a massive lone two-stage lander carrying enough fuel for the return journey.

Instead of one big ship, Apollo would have a separate lunar lander to rendezvous and dock with a command "mothership" in lunar orbit. This approach demanded that Apollo astronauts learn to fly their spacecraft precisely.

A NASA engineer explains Lunar Orbital Rendezvous (LOR)—a complex but weight-saving mission plan.

DOCKING PRACTICE

While preparation began for Apollo, another spacecraft was needed for practice maneuvers in Low Earth Orbit. Gemini was a two-man capsule, retrorockets and a service module that could change orbital altitude. Apollo training began on *Gemini 8* when Neil Armstrong and David Scott docked briefly with an *Agena* Target Vehicle (ATV) on March 16, 1966. Early troubles overcome, *Gemini 10* and *11* successfully docked with their ATVs. New records were also set for spaceflight endurance.

Payload fairing

Gemini 9A was part-aborted when the ATDA (a hastily put-together docking vehicle to replace a lost ATV) failed to shed its payload fairing.

GEMINI SPACECRAFT

1. **REENTRY MODULE** Twin seats
2. **EQUIPMENT MODULE** Fuel cells, battery, oxygen, thrusters
3. **DOCKING ADAPTER** To connect to ATDA
4. **RENDEZVOUS ANTENNA** For locating ATDA
5. **RETROGRADE MODULE** Thrusters to maneuver in orbit and retrorockets for deorbiting

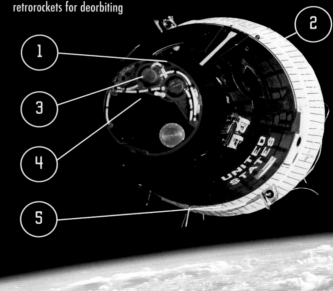

XII

LOVELL ALDRIN

"It looks like an angry alligator rotating around out here."
Gemini 9A astronaut Tom Stafford

ATV

On Gemini 12, Buzz Aldrin spent a total of four and a half hours taking part in Extra Vehicular Activity (EVA)—a spacewalk. The docked ATV is in the background.

The **GEMINI** program cost **$7.3 BILLION** in **2010** dollars. Each **MANNED FLIGHT** had a price tag of $723 million.

APOLLO RAMPS UP

NASA calculated that a Lunar Orbital Rendezvous (LOR) mission would be light enough to launch on a three-stage rocket. Such a rocket was already being developed under Wernher von Braun at the Army Ballistic Missile Agency. So von Braun's Saturn rocket family was adapted for Apollo.

The mothership design had two sections: a pressurized Command/reentry Module, CM, for three crew members, and an unpressurized Service Module, SM, with life support, fuel, and an engine for lunar orbit and the journey home. The Apollo astronaut pool of 32 had Mercury and Gemini veterans as commanders. The first manned Apollo test flight, led by Gus Grissom, with Ed White as senior pilot, and Roger Chaffee as pilot, was set for January 1967.

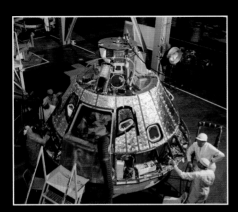

The Apollo Command Capsule for the first manned mission was fabricated at North American Aviation during 1966.

GRISSOM   WHITE   CHAFFEE

The first test crew named their inaugural flight Apollo 1.

PROBING THE MOON

Detailed exploration and mapping of the Moon was essential for Apollo. By 1960 only *Pioneer 4* had flown by, at a lengthy 36,000 miles (58,000 km). NASA had to do better.

MAPPING THE MOON

Ranger was NASA's program to take close-up Moon images. The first six probes were either launch failures, missed their target, or had camera failure. NASA finally succeeded with *Rangers 7* through *9*. Their images showed that "seas", or lunar mares, were ancient and inactive lava flows.

Next came Lunar Orbiters. They used retrorockets to slow as they reached the Moon, allowing them to be captured by its gravity. *Orbiters 1-3* scouted landing sites. *Orbiters 4-5* mapped 99% of the near and far sides.

Ranger 7, launched in 1964, was the first US probe to return detailed images of the Moon. It snapped more than 4,000 pictures before it crashed into the surface.

Camera window

SEA OF VAPORS

OCEAN OF STORMS

Since 1959, more than 70 PROBES have successfully EXPLORED the MOON.

LUNAR ORBITER

1. **DIRECTIONAL ANTENNA**
2. **VELOCITY CONTROL ENGINE**
Also called a retrorocket
3. **REACTION JETS** Nitrogen gas
4. **OMNIDIRECTIONAL ANTENNA**
5. **CAMERA BODY AND SYSTEMS**
Twin camera lenses
6. **SOLAR PANELS**

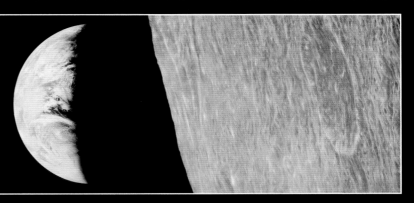

Just before it sped towards the far side on August 23, 1966, Lunar Orbiter 1 captured a stunning image of Earth shadowed by the Moon—a foretaste of wonders to come.

SEA OF SERENITY

SEA OF CRISES

SEA OF TRANQUILITY

Surveyor 3, 1967, was imaged by Apollo 12 in 1969.

SURVEYING THE MOON

On June 2, 1966, the first Surveyor lander touched down on the Moon. It was four months after the Soviet *Luna 9*. *Surveyor 1* transmitted hundreds of black-and-white stereo (3D) TV pictures of its surroundings and took temperature readings.

Each Surveyor probe had a rocket underneath to slow its descent. But this did not always work. *Surveyor 2* hit the surface, while *Surveyor 4* exploded above. The last Surveyors took rock samples, which were mainly volcanic basalt.

The lunar Surveyors took close-up pictures of their landing feet, allowing NASA engineers to assess the depth and composition of the Moon's regolith, or soil.

LANDING SITES

Apollo's plan was that, if the Command/Service Module's engine failed, the mission would abort by swinging around the Moon to slingshot back to Earth. This meant landing sites were limited to a strip along the lunar equator. Terrain flatness and the Sun's angle were also crucial. A spot on the Sea of Tranquility seemed the most promising.

A recent NASA lunar probe is the Lunar Atmosphere and Dust Environment Explorer (LADEE). It analyzes the fragile lunar atmosphere—before human activity may change it, forever.

THE SOVIET MOON EFFORT

Escape rockets

① ② ③ ④ ⑤

In 1965, the Soviet space agency OKB-1 began to develop a huge rocket to take astronauts to the Moon. The sheer scale and cost of the project doomed it to infighting and failure

ZOND SPACECRAFT

N-1/L3 MOON ROCKET

1. **PAYLOAD** 7K-LOK and LK Lander
2. **L3 4TH AND 5TH STAGES** For translunar injection
3. **N-1 3RD STAGE** 4 rockets
4. **N-1 2ND STAGE** 8 rockets
5. **N-1 1ST STAGE** 30 rockets

SOYUZ 7K-LOK

Command/ reentry capsule

Crew area

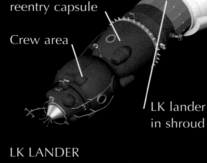

LK lander in shroud

Strutwork

LK LANDER

Egress hatch

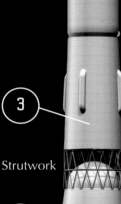

The Soviet moonshot followed the profile of Apollo, with a Soyuz command/reentry ship and a small one-man lander in lunar orbit. This L3 spacecraft would be launched on a monster five-stage rocket—the N1, a design with many problems. Korolev, its designer, died in 1966. It was woefully underfunded and secrecy hampered testing of its rockets and stages.

The first N1 launch exploded at 7.4 miles (12 km). The second exploded at launch. The third rolled out of control on take-off. And the fourth fell in pieces when its engine cut out 25 miles (40 km) up. The Soviet Moon mission had come to a spectacular ending.

The N1 first stage used 30 rockets fed by complex plumbing. It was plagued by quality control and flight stabilization issues.

In a scene that was never to be, the L3 blasts away from Earth. The only Soyuz to ever circle the Moon were unmanned Zond probes.

> *"The Soviets did not have the technology to send a man to the Moon."* — Piers Bizony, Yuri Gagarin biographer

The second N-1 launch destroyed the launch pad complex, in one of the largest man-made non-nuclear explosions ever recorded.

The Soviets had better luck with probes. Luna 9 made the first ever extra-terrestrial soft landing in 1966. It transmitted the first pictures of the lunar surface.

MOONWALKERS

The Soviets planned to send Lunokhod ("Moonwalker") robots to scout sites for manned landings and to act as radio beacons. When the manned Moon program was canceled, these were retasked as remote probes. Landing in the Sea of Rains in November, 1971, *Luna 17* lowered ramps and released *Lunokhod 1*, an eight-wheeled rover the size of a small car. It was controlled by radio from Earth and had an X-ray spectrometer, X-ray telescope, and an array of TV cameras. *Lunokhod 2* in 1973 also had a soil tester and other instruments that would become familiar on NASA's Mars probes two decades later.

Exit ramps

LUNA 17 LANDER

Lunokhod moonwalkers used solar panels to recharge their batteries during the lunar day, and a radioactive Polonium 210 generator for warmth at night.

LUNOKHOD 1   Solar array

Antenna

The **Soviet MOON FIASCO** was only **revealed** when **RUSSIA** adopted **GLASNOST** (**openness**) in the **1980s.**

MISSION: APOLLO

January 27, 1967: tragedy struck *Apollo 1*. A fire broke out in the Command Module during a dry run of the launch countdown. As smoke engulfed their flaming capsule, all three astronauts suffocated.

The Apollo 1 *crew practiced in a simulator capsule eight days before their fatal accident.*

A flammable 100% oxygen atmosphere, and hard-to-open hatch, doomed the crew.

ORBITAL TESTING

Apollo's Command Module was redesigned and launched on unmanned missions. Then *Apollo 7* took off on October 11, 1967. Walter Schirra, Donn Eisele, and Walter Cunningham tested the Command/Service Module, CSM, in Earth orbit. The mission was accomplished, but not without friction between the astronauts and the ground control personnel.

With the Lunar Module (LM) still under construction, Apollo 7 practice-docked to a target positioned in their spent third-stage rocket.

AROUND THE MOON

Apollo's troublesome Lunar Module, LM, was not ready until 1969. Meantime the Soviets had circled the Moon with a Zond probe. Instead of docking with the LM above Earth, *Apollo 8* was sent to orbit the Moon for a thorough test of the CSM's main engine (and to beat any Soviet attempt). The mission was crewed by Commander Frank Borman, with CM pilot Jim Lovell, and LM pilot Bill Anders. A stirring success, the public enjoyed striking images of Earth rising above the Moon as the crew read out Biblical passages on Christmas Eve.

Apollo 8 rolled out on its mobile launch platform at Kennedy Space Center, Florida, in December, 1968. It was the first manned Saturn V launch.

Apollo 8 made ten Moon orbits, revealing detailed images of the cratered surface.

Anders, Lovell, and Borman were the first humans to leave Earth orbit.

Apollo 9's 10-day mission included two spacewalks. Here Scott stands in the open hatchway of CSM "Gumdrop". Photographer Schweickart was standing on the hatchway of LM "Spider".

LM SHAKEDOWN

On March 9, 1969, a Saturn V finally lifted off with a complete man-rated Apollo spacecraft onboard. *Apollo 9* was commanded by James McDivitt, with CM pilot David Scott, and LM pilot Rusty Schweickart. They practiced rendezvous and docking between the CSM and a fully-powered LM in Low Earth Orbit. Schweickart, suffering from space sickness, fired up the LM's descent and ascent engines. He also tested the life support backpacks that would be used on the Moon.

DRESS REHEARSAL

Five and a half weeks after *Apollo 9*, *Apollo 10* blasted away from Earth orbit and journeyed to the Moon. The veteran crew—commander Thomas Stafford, CM pilot John Young, and LM pilot Eugene Cernan—enacted every part of a real landing—except Moon touchdown.

The mission went like clockwork until LM descent stage separation, 10 miles (16 km) above the Moon. Repeated thruster blasts sent the ascent stage rolling alarmingly. Stafford and Cernan regained control and redocked with Young, bringing detailed images of the landing site for future missions.

Docking probe

Apollo 10's view from its LM shows "Snoopy" shortly after separating from CSM "Charlie Brown" (Snoopy's owner), high above the lunar surface, on May 22, 1969.

400,000 people were **INVOLVED** in **BRINGING** the **11**-year **APOLLO Program** to **FRUITION.**

Having jettisoned its descent stage, the LM "Snoopy" ascent stage powers up for docking, viewed by CM pilot John Young.

APOLLO: SATURN V

The three-stage Saturn V was as tall as a 30-story building and capable of lifting more than 53 tons. It remains the most powerful space rocket ever built.

Apollo 7 rode into space on a Saturn IB, which used the powerful S-IV as a second stage.

ACCELERATED TESTING

The Moon rocket had five huge F-1 first-stage engines fueled by liquid oxygen (LOX) and kerosene. The second stage was powered by five smaller J-2 engines burning LOX and liquid hydrogen (LH2). The third stage single J-2 engine was designed to be restartable in space.

Huge rockets like the F-1 were prone to unstable burning. It took seven years and the destruction of many test engines before NASA engineers were able to tune the F-1 to self-damp (cancel out) combustion instability. Early versions of the CSM and LM were launched on smaller Saturn rockets with the third stage. The first complete Saturn V—with unmanned Apollo 4—was tested "all up" on November 9, 1967. With a thunderous roar, it lifted off and performed... flawlessly.

The second test launch, Apollo 6, was marred by dangerous vibrations in the J-2 engines which ruptured fuel lines.

SATURN V ROCKET

1. **ESCAPE TOWER** Rockets to pull the CM to safety in a launch abort
2. **PAYLOAD** Apollo CSM and LM
3. **S-IV** Third stage: 66,770 gallons (252,750 liters) liquid hydrogen (LH2), 19,359 gallons (73,280 liters) LOX
4. **S-II** Second stage: 260,000 gallons (984,200 liters) LH2, 80,000 gallons (303,000 liters) LOX
5. **S-IC** First stage: 318,000 gallons (1,204,000 liters) LOX, 203,400 gallons (770,000 liters) RP-1 (rocket grade kerosene)

The first stage S-IC LOX tank was lowered onto its RP-1 fuel tank during the manufacture of Saturn V. The design and final assembly of the rocket was overseen by Wernher von Braun (left).

Instrument Unit

Inter-stage adapter

RP-1 tank

Fins

F-1 engines

This Saturn V Instrument Unit awaits installation at Marshall Spaceflight Center. It was the only component directly manufactured by NASA.

SATURN V S-IVB

1. **J-2 ENGINE** Burning LH2/LOX
2. **FUSELAGE** Featuring forward and aft skirts (overhangs)
3. **LUNAR MODULE** Folded unmanned inside LM adapter
4. **SERVICE MODULE** Mated to LM adapter, engine concealed
5. **COMMAND MODULE** Mated to SM

COMPUTER "BRAIN"

The four outer engines on the S-IC and S-II stages were mounted on moveable hydraulics (gimbals). These were controlled by an internal guidance system in an Instrument Unit (IU) located between the third stage and payload.

The IU was the entire vehicle's "brain". It included a digital computer, telemetry instruments, and radio communications. The fuselage of the rocket, even the launch tower, was test-shaken to destruction. Engineers worked quickly to fix the pogo (bouncing) oscillations in the upper stages that threatened the second flight. The third flight shot *Apollo 8* successfully around the Moon.

> The **SATURN V** was **designed** to be **99% RELIABLE**—and **SUCCEEDED**.

LM adapter

The last Apollo Saturn V rose into the night lifting Apollo 17. *The payloads for the later missions were 45% heavier than Apollo 11. In all, 13 Saturn Vs were launched—with no losses.*

The S-II's fairing detached to fall and burn in Earth's outer atmosphere, as its five J-2 rockets boosted Apollo into orbit.

APOLLO: COMMAND/SERVICE MODULE

The CSM was two spacecraft in one—a control ship, joined with a flight ship that housed a powerful engine and life support equipment for the long flight.

The CM had five double-layer, reinforced windows, with inner glass specially coated to filter harmful ultraviolet rays. The windows either side of the hatch had calibration marks to aid docking.

SIM

Later Apollo CSMs scanned the Moon using a Scientific Instrument Module (SIM).

COMMAND SHIP

The command module (CM) was divided into three parts. The forward compartment housed a docking hatch, Earth Landing System (ELS—two drogue and three main parachutes), and two attitude thrusters. The crew compartment had three couches, main instrument panel, and supply storage. A shallow aft compartment housed 10 attitude thrusters and gas bottles. After launch the CM pilot, seated center, flew the ship, with commander seated left, and LM pilot, right.

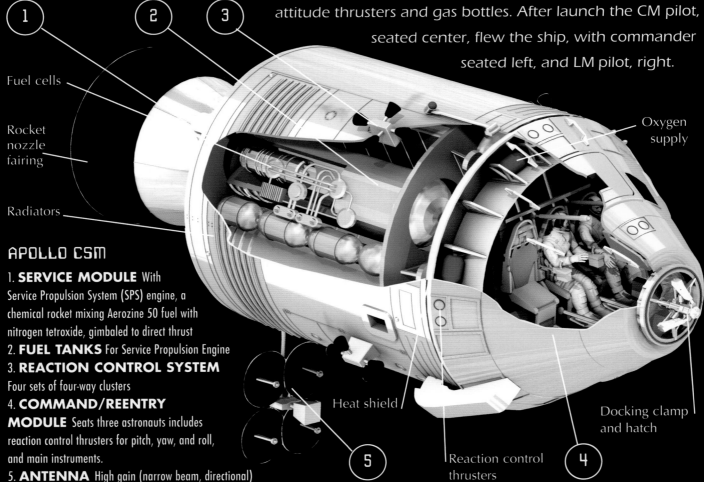

Fuel cells

Rocket nozzle fairing

Radiators

Oxygen supply

Heat shield

Docking clamp and hatch

Reaction control thrusters

APOLLO CSM

1. **SERVICE MODULE** With Service Propulsion System (SPS) engine, a chemical rocket mixing Aerozine 50 fuel with nitrogen tetroxide, gimbaled to direct thrust
2. **FUEL TANKS** For Service Propulsion Engine
3. **REACTION CONTROL SYSTEM** Four sets of four-way clusters
4. **COMMAND/REENTRY MODULE** Seats three astronauts includes reaction control thrusters for pitch, yaw, and roll, and main instruments.
5. **ANTENNA** High gain (narrow beam, directional)

The interior of the CM was designed for long-endurance flight. The seat of the middle couch could be folded to allow standing.

REENTRY POD

Upon return to Earth, the CM separated from the SM and entered the atmosphere. The front of the CM was covered with a braised steel honeycomb mesh filled with reinforced (epoxy) plastic, designed to be ablative—char and vaporize, carrying heat away. Protecting the rear of the CM was a large circular

Sheathed in protective plastic, the Apollo CSM was lowered onto the Instrument Unit "brain".

ablative heat shield. This took the brunt of the 5,000 °F (2,760 °C) friction heat generated as the craft, angled 45° base-first, skidded into the atmosphere at 25,000 miles (40,230 km) per hour.

Once slowed enough, the nose heat shield popped off, deploying the chute landing systems. Weak metal ribs in the rear CM compartment deformed on impact with the sea.

Apollo astronauts practiced opening the docking hatch in the Command Module nose.

The **CM** was **designed** to land **SAFELY** on **only TWO parachutes**, as **HAPPENED** on **APOLLO 15**.

Floatation bags

(Right) Apollo capsules, carefully engineered to float, were tracked as they approached splashdown. (Left) The Apollo 8 CM, winched aboard a recovery ship, has its shiny insulating foil skin burnt away.

APOLLO: LUNAR MODULE

The Lunar Module, LM, like the CSM, was a two-in-one spacecraft. The descent stage for landing on the Moon was topped with an ascent stage for leaving the Moon.

THE FIRST PURE SPACECRAFT

The LM descent stage was shaped like a cross, with four propellant tanks fixed around a central variable-thrust rocket. Around this was a skirt with cantilevered struts at four corners. The struts had honeycomb cores that crushed on landing to level the weight of the module on uneven ground.

The ascent stage was built around a fixed-thrust rocket with a cylindrical pressure cabin on top, and two propellant tanks. Four thrusters provided attitude control. Equipment and systems were mounted inside and out, giving the ascent stage an ungainly, bulky look. This did not matter—the LM operated only in the vacuum of space.

The Apollo EVA (Extra Vehicular Activity) spacesuit comprised a water-cooled undergarment, a multi-layered pressure suit, and a protective outer suit coated with teflon.

Astronauts were trained on the Lunar Landing Research Vehicle (LLRV), to simulate the difficulties of landing in the Moon's low gravity.

Breathing oxygen tank

Fuel tank

Ascent engine nozzle

Cabin

Ascent engine oxidizer tank

As the Apollo 9 ascent stage drifted in space, it showed the engine and its uneven fuel and oxidizer tanks (oxidizer being heavier than fuel)

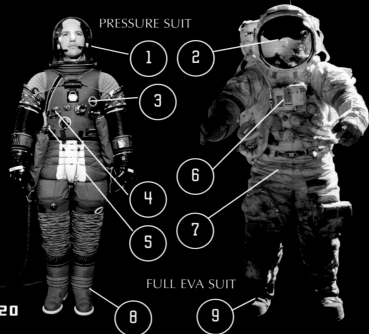

PRESSURE SUIT

1 2

3

6

4

5 7

FULL EVA SUIT

8 9

APOLLO SPACESUIT

1. **PRESSURE HELMET**
2. **OUTER HELMET** Gold tinted visor
3. **PLSS WATER SUPPLY** In-suit climate
4. **EMERGENCY OXYGEN PURGE**
5. **PLSS OXYGEN SUPPLY**
6. **PLSS CHEST CONTROLLER**
7. **MULTI-LAYER EVA GARMENT**
Thermal, micrometeoroid protection for outside work
8. **INNER BOOT**
9. **OVERSHOE**

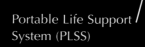

Portable Life Support System (PLSS)

Crew practiced in an LM simulator. With no seats, they stood up—which gave a better view through the windows.

> **"The LM descent engine was Apollo's most outstanding technical development."**
> *Chariots for Apollo, NASA*

ADDED COMPLEXITY

Designing and fabricating a vehicle to land on the Moon safely, and also act as a shelter and escape craft, was the most challenging task on Apollo. An adjustable-thrust rocket had never been made for spaceflight. The odd-angled shape of the crew cabin, with small windows angled down for landing view, had to be both welded and riveted. The astronauts themselves helped to design the cockpit layout, with duplicated flight controls for safety.

LUNAR MODULE

1. **RENDEZVOUS RADAR**
2. **ASCENT MODULE**
3. **DIRECTIONAL ANTENNA**
4. **REACTION CONTROL SYSTEM**
Four-engine cluster
5. **DESCENT MODULE**

Deflection baffle

Descent engine

Gold insulation

Egress ramp

The **LM'S aluminum LADDER** was so **LIGHT** that **it** would **CRUMPLE** if **USED** in **Earth's GRAVITY.**

APOLLO 11

On July 16, 1969, nearly one million people gathered at the launch site to watch *Apollo 11* lift off. Around the globe almost a billion watched on TV, willing the astronauts to reach the Moon safely.

Onlookers collectively held their breath as the giant rocket took 12 seconds to clear the tower.

MICHAEL COLLINS

Commander Neil Armstrong, CM pilot Michael Collins, and LM pilot Buzz Aldrin carried their personal life support packs to the pad. All three were veterans of Gemini.

"LIFT-OFF! WE HAVE A LIFT-OFF!"

"Six, five, four, three..." In the Saturn V, turbo pumps sped up, forcing propellant at the rate of 9,920 pounds (4,500 kg) a second into *Apollo 11*'s F-1 engines. These reached 90% of thrust... "...Two, one..." Launch commitment, and enormous clamps holding the rocket down released.

As *Apollo 11* cleared the tower, its internal guidance computer rolled it toward a Low Earth Orbit trajectory. At 300 seconds, the first stage burned out. Moments later, the escape tower blasted away. In six minutes they reached orbit. "Shutdown," said Armstrong.

At 42 miles (67 km) up, small rockets forced away the spent Saturn S-IC stage. It tumbled down into the ocean.

Two hours 15 minutes after launch, the S-VIB's engine re-ignited and burned for six minutes, propelling Apollo 11 away from Earth.

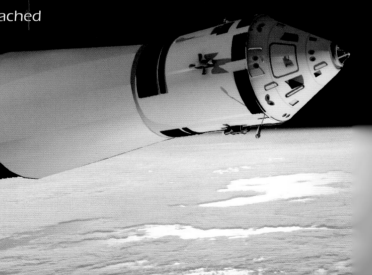

> *"The Moon I have known all my life has been replaced by the most awesome sphere I have ever seen."*
>

Thirty minutes into Trans Lunar Injection (TLI), the LM adapter covers blew away. CM pilot Collins maneuvered the CSM around to dock with the LM.

"EAGLE, YOU'RE GO FOR LANDING..."

Collins guided the CSM docking probe home and released the LM from the rocket stage. A three-second engine pulse moved them clear. The Apollo spacecraft was turned to stand on its engine and spun slowly like a top.

Three days later, July 19, Collins fired the engine for six minutes to brake them so they could be grabbed by the Moon's gravity. Another burn of 17 seconds circularized their orbit at 60 miles (96 km) above the moon. On July 20, LM "Eagle" undocked from CSM "Columbia". "The Eagle has wings," radioed Armstrong. Mission Control cleared for landing. It took 12 minutes to reach the surface.

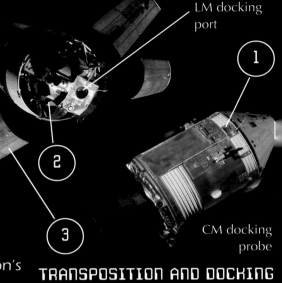

LM docking port

CM docking probe

TRANSPOSITION AND DOCKING

1. **CSM "COLUMBIA"** Reaction control engines maneuvered it around to face LM
2. **LM "EAGLE"** Folded inside Saturn S-IVB third stage
3. **LM adapter** Separated from S-IV with propellant charges

APOLLO 11's guidance **computer** was on a **PAR with** the **ELECTRONICS** in a **modern-day TOASTER.**

Landing probes

Armstrong fired a 30-second burn on the "Eagle" descent engine to head down to the surface.

Buzz Aldrin inside the LM. The Apollo commander flew the ship down. The LM pilot monitored altitude, fuel levels, and systems on the descent.

"ONE SMALL STEP..."

Apollo 11's LM headed toward a crater slope dotted with boulders. Armstrong adjusted attitude and speed, and hovered past the crater. Dust flared as the ground rushed up. "Contact light," called out Aldrin.

Armstrong's step off the ladder onto the lunar surface was captured by a camera on the lander. The moment was broadcast across the world.

Onboard "Columbia" Collins had listened in to the landing with bated breath.

"..THE EAGLE HAS LANDED..."

They had landed, with barely 20 seconds' descent fuel remaining, somewhere in the Sea of Tranquility. After food and a brief rest, Armstrong and Aldrin carefully suited up. It took 45 minutes to depressurize the cabin. Aldrin helped guide his commander through the egress hatch. "That's one small step for [a] man, one giant leap for mankind," said Armstrong, as his boot touched the surface. The ground was powdery, like charcoal dust. There was much to do and very little time.

Aldrin was photographed by Armstrong as he descended the ladder. The Moon has one-sixth of Earth's gravity, making movements easy.

The **sticky LUNAR SOIL** is **made** from **EONS** of meteorite **IMPACTS** ground to a **FINE POWDER.**

"Beautiful, beautiful. Magnificent desolation..."
Astronaut Buzz Aldrin, on stepping out of the LM

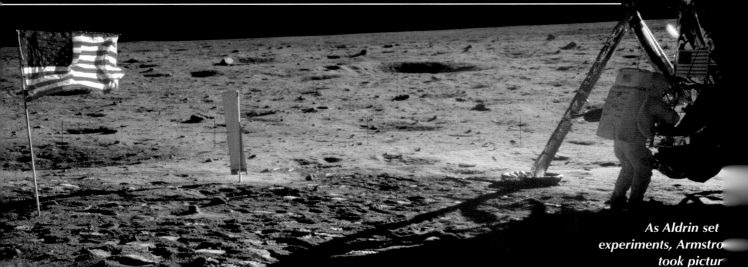

As Aldrin set experiments, Armstro[ng] took pictur[es]

"..IT'S VERY PRETTY OUT HERE.."

The two moonwalkers unveiled a plaque on the LM, performed a flag-raising ceremony, and took a call from US President Nixon. Putting aside his awe of their surroundings, Aldrin removed the science package from the descent module. Atmospheric and seismic instruments deployed, and moon rocks gathered, the crew returned to "Eagle."

They lifted off 21 hours after landing. Reuniting with the CSM, the LM was cast away. Collins lit up the engine to propel them Earthwards, to a successful reentry.

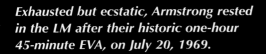

Exhausted but ecstatic, Armstrong rested in the LM after their historic one-hour 45-minute EVA, on July 20, 1969.

The astronauts wore bio-suit[s] on arrival at Earth. They spen[t] three weeks in quarantine before at last receiving a[ ]heroes' welcome[ ](below)

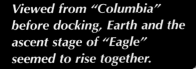

Viewed from "Columbia" before docking, Earth and the ascent stage of "Eagle" seemed to rise together.

DISASTER IN SPACE

By the time of *Apollo 13*, going to the Moon was beginning to appear routine. But CSM "Odyssey" would place its crew in mortal danger and test NASA's ingenuity to the limit.

Apollo 13 lifted off on April 11, 1970. Veteran commander Jim Lovell, CM pilot Jack Swigert, and LM pilot Fred Haise were heading for the geologically interesting Fra Mauro area of the Moon.

JIM
LOVELL

FRED
HAISE

JACK
SWIGERT

Apart from lightning striking the Saturn V during launch, Apollo 12 (November 14-24, 1969) went like clockwork. LM "Intrepid" touched down in the Sea of Storms near the site of the 1967's lander Surveyor 3.

The explosion in oxygen tank 2 ruptured the line from oxygen tank 1. This caused the loss of the entire CSM oxygen supply and led to the shutdown of all its fuel cells.

"HOUSTON, WE HAVE A PROBLEM..."

Apollo 13 was 200,000 miles (320,000 km) from Earth when Mission Control asked Swigert to do a routine stir of the oxygen tanks. There was a loud thump. Dials showed loss of oxygen and power. "We are venting something out into space," reported Lovell, as he looked out the window. It was their oxygen.

As the CM "Odyssey" batteries drained, the crew transferred to the LM "Aquarius". Houston calculated the burn needed on the LM descent engine to swing them around the Moon and back to Earth. It was mission aborted, and a free return trajectory.

Lovell floated in the cold cabin of "Aquarius". The LM had more than enough oxygen but the crew needed to carefully conserve its battery power and water.

Alan Shepard (who nearly commanded Apollo 13) listened intently as the crew discussed how to keep their air breathable for the duration of the flight.

The **unfolding DRAMA** featured **DAILY** on **TV**—with **reentry** as the **ultimate CLIFFHANGER.**

The crippled Apollo 13 spacecraft rounded the far side of the Moon. Another long engine burn was needed from "Aquarius" when Earth became visible.

AROUND THE MOON

Rounding the Moon, the stricken craft needed to point toward Earth before the burn. The swarm of debris traveling with it made navigating by stars impossible. Over a tense few minutes, Lovell guided Swigert in manual alignment using the Sun. The CM had long been powered down after charging its batteries. Near Earth, cold and damp, the CM was switched back on. Luckily it did not short-circuit.

The crew jettisoned the damaged SM and then moved from LM "Aquarius" to the CM, before saying goodbye to their "lunar lifeboat". Below, Houston waited agonizingly through the reentry, wondering if the accident had damaged the CM's heat shield.

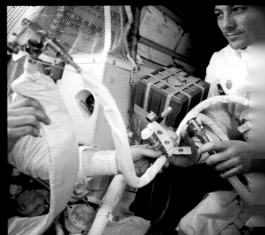

Rising carbon dioxide levels forced the crew to re-rig fittings on unused filters from the LM, which had differently shaped openings to those on the CM.

Apollo 13, safely home at last.

On April 17, mission controllers in Houston watched the Apollo 13 capsule descend on its parachutes. The Moon landing was lost. But returning the astronauts safely to Earth was a triumph of creative engineering and human fortitude.

APOLLO: FINAL MISSIONS

Launched on January 31, 1971, *Apollo 14* was tasked with fulfilling *Apollo 13's* lost mission. For *Apollos 15-17*, NASA devised more science experiments and an enhanced Lunar Module.

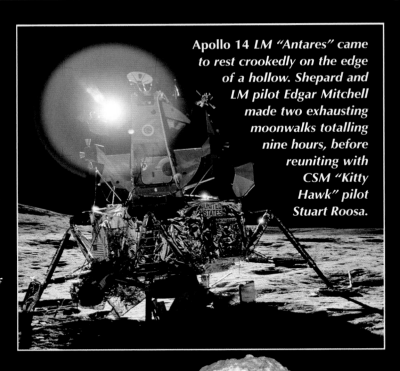

Apollo 14 LM "Antares" came to rest crookedly on the edge of a hollow. Shepard and LM pilot Edgar Mitchell made two exhausting moonwalks totalling nine hours, before reuniting with CSM "Kitty Hawk" pilot Stuart Roosa.

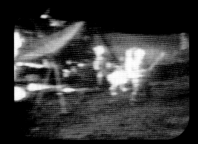

At 47 years old, Apollo 14 *commander Alan Shepard was the oldest Moon visitor. After his second moonwalk, Shepard hit a couple of golf balls with a club made from lunar tools.*

ROAMING AND ROVING

Apollo 14 spent 33 hours on the Moon. For *Apollo* 15, the Extended Lunar Module (ELM) "Falcon" featured an uprated descent engine to help carry a folded Lunar Roving Vehicle (LRV) or "Moon buggy". The addition of a cabin toilet allowed the crew to spend 75 hours on the Moon.

Commander David Scott and LM pilot James Irwin landed "Falcon" on August 7, 1971, in the Sea of Rains. On CSM "Endeavour" pilot Alfred Worden scanned the Moon using new sensors.

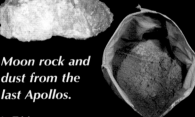

Moon rock and dust from the last Apollos.

LRV

1. **DIRECTIONAL ANTENNA**
2. **WIDE BEAM ANTENNA**
3. **COLOR TV CAMERA**
4. **BATTERIES** Between wheels
5. **TOOLS CARRIER**

Apollo 15 set a new record of 18¹/₂ hours outside spread over three moonwalks.

Mesh wheels
Instrument panel

> *"We leave the Moon as we came and, God willing, we shall return."*
> — Gene Cernan, *Apollo* 17

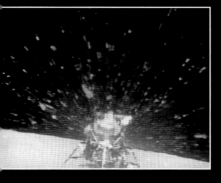

Apollo 16 *LM "Orion" ascent stage blasted away from the descent stage on April 24, 1972. Commander John Young and LM pilot Charles Duke were the first to visit the Moon's mountains.*

The APOLLO program cost $150 BILLION in today's dollars—$50 BILLION less than the SPACE SHUTTLE.

GOODBYE TO THE MOON

As with all later Apollo missions, *Apollo 16* CM "Casper" pilot Ken Mattingly spacewalked to retrieve science data from the Scientific Instrument Module. *Apollo 17* included the first qualified scientist, LM pilot Harrison Schmitt. A geologist, he descended with commander Gene Cernan to Taurus-Littrow on December 11, 1972. Schmitt took core samples and studied lunar bedrock with a variety of instruments. During their 75 hours on the Moon, they drove a total distance of 22 miles (35.4 km) in the LRV.

APOLLO 17 CSM "AMERICA"

On December 14, 1972, Cernan and Schmitt rose in LM "Challenger" for the last-ever Apollo lunar rendezvous and docking, with CM pilot Ron Evans onboard "America".

A wistful-looking Gene Cernan clowned with Harrison Schmitt on their journey to the Moon. After Apollo, NASA missions stayed resolutely in Low Earth Orbit.

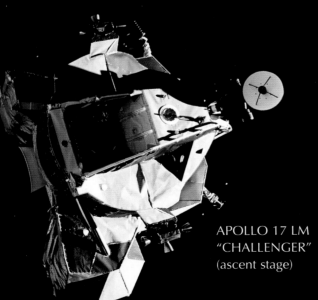

APOLLO 17 LM "CHALLENGER" (ascent stage)

The last man on the Moon saluted the US flag. In his final speech, Cernan said: "America's challenge of today has forged man's destiny of tomorrow…" One of Apollo's biggest legacies was inspiring future generations of astronauts and scientists.

TECH FILES – LUNAR EXPLORATION

PROBES (PRIOR TO APOLLO)

LUNA 1 SOVIET LAUNCHED: January 2, 1959 **Mission:** Lunar flyby (failed impact) **Science:** Magnetometer, Geiger counter, scintillation counter, and micrometeorite detector

PIONEER 4 US LAUNCHED: March 3, 1959 **Mission:** Lunar flyby and heliocentric orbit **Science:** Photoelectric sensor to trigger camera (failed), Geiger–Müller tubes

LUNA 3 SOVIET LAUNCHED: October 4, 1959 **Mission:** Lunar flyby and planetary science **Science:** Yenisey-2 imaging system, micrometeoroid and cosmic ray detectors

RANGER 7 US LAUNCHED: July 28, 1964 **Mission:** Lunar impactor **Science:** Six television vidicon cameras

LUNAR ORBITER 1 US LAUNCHED: August 10, 1966 **Mission:** Mapping and science **Science:** Twin cameras, selenodesy (Moon mapping), radiation and micrometeoroid detectors

UNMANNED LANDERS AND ROVERS

SURVEYOR 1 US LAUNCHED: May 30, 1966 **Mission:** Achieve first ever soft lunar landing **Science:** Television vidicon camera

LUNOKHOD 1 SOVIET LAUNCHED: November 10, 1970 **Mission:** First ever roving remote-controlled robot on another celestial body **Science:** Four television cameras, lunar soil testers, X-ray spectrometer, X-ray telescope, cosmic ray detectors, laser device

LUNOKHOD 2 SOVIET LAUNCHED: January 11, 1973 **Mission:** Roving remote-controlled robot **Science:** Three television cameras, four panoramic cameras, soil mechanics tester, solar X-ray experiment, astrophotometer to measure visible and ultraviolet light, magnetometer, radiometer, photodetector, laser corner reflector

HUMAN EXPLORATION

APOLLO 8 US LAUNCHED: December 21, 1968 **Mission:** First ever manned lunar flyby – Commander Frank Borman, CSM Pilot James Lovell, LM Pilot William Anders

APOLLO 10 US LAUNCHED: May 18, 1969 **Mission:** Dress rehearsal for Apollo 11 – Commander Thomas Stafford, CSM Pilot John Young, LM Pilot Eugene Cernan

APOLLO 11 US LAUNCHED: July 16, 1969 **Mission:** First ever human landing on the Moon – Commander Neil Armstrong, CSM Pilot Michael Collins, LM Pilot Edwin "Buzz" Aldrin, Jr **Science:** Multiple cameras, lunar Laser Ranging Experiment and Passive Lunar Seismic Experiment (PLSE)

APOLLO 12 US LAUNCHED: November 14, 1969 **Mission:** Precision landing with two-day stay, two moonwalks – Commander Charles "Pete" Conrad, Jr., CSM Pilot Richard Gordon, Jr., LM Pilot Alan Bean **Science:** Color TV camera (damaged), Apollo Lunar Surface Experiments Package (ALSEP) station, PLSE, tri-axis magnetometer, solar wind ion detection, low-energy solar wind, Active Lunar Seismic Experiment (ALSE)

APOLLO 13 US LAUNCHED: April 17, 1970 **Mission:** Mission aborted to lunar swingby, LM used as "lifeboat" spacecraft – Commander James Lovell, CSM Pilot Jack Swigert, LM Pilot Fred Haise

APOLLO 14 US LAUNCHED: January 31, 1971 **Mission:** Two-day stay, two moonwalks and use of Modular Equipment Transporter – Commander Alan Shepard, Jr., CSM Pilot Stuart Roosa, LM Pilot Edgar Mitchell **Science:** Color TV camera, ALSEP station including new seismic studies, first US materials processing experiments in space

APOLLO 15 US LAUNCHED: July 26, 1971 **Mission:** Three-day stay using Extended LM, three moonwalks and Lunar Roving Vehicle – Commander David Scott, CSM Pilot Alfred Worden, LM Pilot James Irwin **Science:** Scientific Instrument Module (SIM) on CSM

APOLLO 16 US LAUNCHED: April 16, 1972 **Mission:** Three-day stay using Extended LM, three moonwalks and Lunar Roving Vehicle – Commander John Young, CSM Pilot Thomas Mattingly II, LM Pilot Charles Duke, Jr. **Science:** SIM, ALSEP, Far Ultraviolet Camera/Spectrograph (FUC/S), core samples

APOLLO 17 US LAUNCHED: December 7, 1972 **Mission:** Three-day stay using Extended LM, three moonwalks and Lunar Roving Vehicle – Commander Eugene Cernan, CSM Pilot Ronald Evans, LM Pilot Harrison Schmitt **Science:** Enhanced SIM, ALSEP, FUC/S, Surface Electrical Properties (SEP) experiment, core samples

GLOSSARY

ATMOSPHERE layer of gases around a space object such as a planet

CM Command/reentry Module of the *Apollo* spacecraft, where the astronauts lived and worked, and which came back to Earth's surface. For most of the mission it was joined to the SM, Service Module

CSM The joined-together Command/reentry Module (see above) and Service Module (see below) of the *Apollo* spacecraft

DESCENT STAGE lower part of the Lunar Module that fired its rocket to slow down and land on the Moon's surface, and which was left behind when the ascent stage took off

EGRESS HATCH opening to leave a spacecraft through, especially in an emergency, and come back in again

GRAVITY force of attraction between objects, which is especially huge for massive objects like planets and stars

LM Lunar Module, part of the Apollo spacecraft that detached from the CSM (see above) and landed on the Moon's surface

MOON space object that orbits a planet. The single moon of Earth is usually known as the Moon (capital letter M)

ORBIT regular path of one object around a larger one, determined by the speed, mass, and gravity of the objects

PLANET large space object that has a spherical shape due to its gravity, and has cleared a regular orbital path around a star

SATELLITE space object that goes around or orbits another, including natural satellites like the Moon orbiting Earth or Earth orbiting the Sun, and man-made satellites like *Apollo* orbiting Earth or the Moon

SM Service Module, unpressurized part of the *Apollo* spacecraft, containing mainly equipment and systems

INDEX